"This is a beautifully illustrated, succinct collection of short stories that can help young children gain insight into acceptable and unacceptable physical contact. Teaching any child how to self-advocate can be tricky, however Hunter Manasco's *An Exceptional Children's Guide to Touch* provides wonderful visual instructions and a gateway for discussion about this delicate subject. Child maltreatment is endemic, and I applaud Manasco's matter-of-fact presentation of this topic. His book speaks to the needs of all young children and vulnerable adults trying to navigate their way through our complex and confusing sexual jungle. *An Exceptional Children's Guide to Touch* is an excellent resource for parents, teachers, and other adults working with young children and exceptional people."

—*Jane Whelen Banks, MHSt, FNP, author of* The Lovable Liam Series

"This superbly crafted book teaches the child with special needs about the complexity of touching without denying them the affection and reassurance that touch can give. Its child-friendly language and illustrations are perfect for explaining inappropriate touch without being frightening or embarrassing. In a nutshell, it provides clear and simple guidelines, backed up by the reassurance that a trusted adult is always on hand to help if there is any confusion. This book cannot fail to touch a chord with parents and professionals alike in its exceptionally brilliant simplicity."

—*K.I. Al-Ghani, experienced specialist advisory teacher, autism trainer and author of* The Red Beast

"*An Exceptional Children's Guide to Touch* will be of great use to anyone involved with children that have any learning or development need. The combined use of Hunter's text and Katharine's illustrations has created a wonderful resource to help navigate the complexities of social rules and norms regarding physical interactions, traditionally a sensitive area to broach. This book could be used with an individual child or within a group setting and would be a valuable addition to all parents', carers', and professionals' libraries."

—*Jackie Bateman, child protection specialist (sexually harmful behaviour) and children's services manager, Barnardo's* The Junction

of related interest

Liam Says "Hi"
Learning to Greet a Friend
Jane Whelen Banks
ISBN 978 1 84310 901 3
eISBN 978 1 84642 873 9
Part of The Lovable Liam Series

Caring for Myself
A Social Skills Storybook
Christy Gast and Jane Krug
Photographs by Kotoe Laackman
ISBN 978 1 84310 872 6
eISBN 978 1 84642 723 7

Different Croaks for Different Folks
All About Children with Special Learning Needs
Midori Ochiai
Illustrated by Hiroko Fujiwara
Translated by Esther Sanders
ISBN 978 1 84310 392 9
eISBN 978 1 84642 467 0

Frog's Breathtaking Speech
How Children (and Frogs) Can Use the Breath to Deal with Anxiety, Anger and Tension
Michael Chissick
Illustrated by Sarah Peacock
ISBN 978 1 84819 091 7
eISBN 978 0 85701 074 2

The Red Beast
Controlling Anger in Children with Asperger's Syndrome
K.I. Al-Ghani
Illustrated by Haitham Al-Ghani
ISBN 978 1 84310 943 3
eISBN 978 1 84642 848 7

Autistic Planet
Jennifer Elder
Illustrated by Marc Thomas and Jennifer Elder
ISBN 978 1 84310 842 9
eISBN 978 1 84642 650 6

An Exceptional Children's Guide to Touch

Teaching Social and Physical Boundaries to Kids

Hunter Manasco   Illustrated by Katharine Manasco

Jessica Kingsley *Publishers*
London and Philadelphia

First published in 2012
by Jessica Kingsley Publishers
116 Pentonville Road
London N1 9JB, UK
and
400 Market Street, Suite 400
Philadelphia, PA 19106, USA

www.jkp.com

Library of Congress Cataloging in Publication Data
Manasco, Hunter.
  An exceptional children's guide to touch : teaching social and physical boundaries to kids / Hunter Manasco ; illustrated by Katharine Manasco.
     p. cm.
  Includes bibliographical references.
  ISBN 978-1-84905-871-1 (alk. paper)
  1. Touch--Juvenile literature. I. Title.
  BF275.M36 2012
  649'.65--dc23

                                2012003491

British Library Cataloguing in Publication Data
A CIP catalogue record for this book is available from the British Library

ISBN 978 1 84905 871 1
eISBN 978 0 85700 659 2

Printed and bound in India

Letter from the Author

Shortly after I began working with children I became aware of the many dangers and social difficulties that children with special needs encounter in their daily lives. The worst of these problems usually involves a child's lack of knowledge or misunderstanding of social rules and norms regarding physical interactions between and among other people. This is a topic that often weighs heavy on the minds of individuals who care for children with special needs. The concerns of these caregivers are well justified. Within months of beginning my work with children, I saw a young student with autism profoundly alienate herself from her peers simply by picking her nose constantly in a certain class (it was a sign of anxiety). I saw the inappropriate hugging behavior of a young woman (they said "it was cute when she was little") become problematic in high school as parents and school officials realized (too late) that this behavior increased this young woman's odds of engaging in inappropriate sexual activity or, at worst, suffering some form of abuse. I saw children with special needs hurt others and be hurt by their peers and caregivers without ever knowing that anything was awry or that something should or could be done about it. I saw all these situations and more, which centered on issues of physical touch and a lack of knowledge or misunderstanding on the part of the child of what was acceptable and what was not acceptable and possibly even problematic. For the parents, caregivers, teachers, and other professionals working with children with special needs, these issues arise often. Yet, when I searched for the materials needed to address these problems I found little or no resources tailored to fit the cognitive and communicative needs of these children. So this book was borne out of a necessity to educate the smallest and most vulnerable members of our population. It should be acknowledged more often that to make our children safe and successful later in life we must keep them safe and successful early in life.

Contents

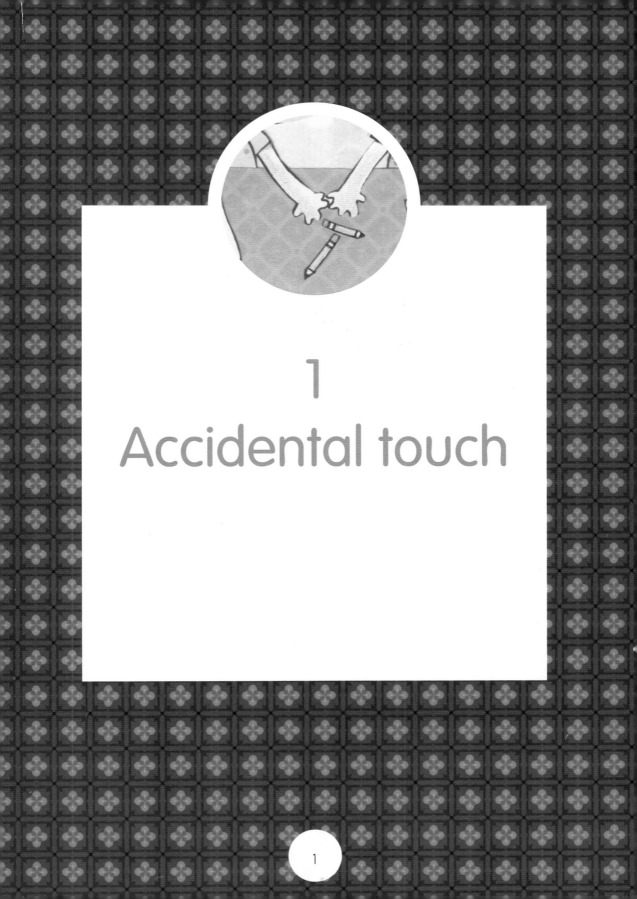

1
Accidental touch

Accidental touch might happen anytime and anywhere. Accidental touch is when someone touches me but does not mean to touch me.

Or when I touch someone else
when I don't mean to.

If someone touches me by accident
that is okay if it does not hurt.

If it hurts I should tell my parent, my
teacher, or another adult all about it
so they can make sure I'm okay.

Sometimes I might touch someone else by accident.

If I touch someone by accident it is probably okay.
I can say, "I'm sorry," or I can say, "Excuse me."

I'm sorry.

But if I hurt someone by accident I should probably say, "I'm sorry." Then I need to tell my parent, my teacher, or another adult right away.

2
Friendly touch

Sometimes people touch each other
to show they care about each
other. This is friendly touch.

Here are some
places friends
touch each other.

Friends usually do not touch any part of my body that is covered by my swimsuit when I go swimming.

If anyone touches me in any of these places I need to tell my parent, my teacher, or another adult right away.

Here are some ways friends may
touch each other.

A hug is also a friendly touch. A hug
is a VERY friendly touch. I should only
hug people I know VERY well.

Most people don't want to be hugged. Most people are happy to shake my hand instead.

Friendly touching never hurts or
makes me feel uncomfortable.

If someone touches me and it hurts or makes me feel bad then they are not being nice and I should tell my parent, my teacher, or another adult all about it.

If someone touches me and it makes me
confused, or if I'm not sure if they are
being nice or not, I should tell my parent,
my teacher, or another adult right away.

3
Hurtful touch

Hurtful touch is usually painful
and often feels bad.

Sometimes, hurtful touch may be confusing.

If I'm confused about someone touching me I should tell my parent, my teacher, or another adult all about it.

Here are some kinds of hurtful touch.

There are lots of other kinds, too.

No one should ever hurt
me or try to hurt me.

If anyone hurts me or tries to hurt me the best thing to do is get away and tell my parent, my teacher, or another adult all about it.

If I hurt somebody I should probably say,
"I'm sorry." Then I should tell my parent, my
teacher, or another adult all about it so that
they can make sure the person I hurt is okay.

4
Touching myself

If I am all alone I can touch myself
anywhere I want to.

I am usually all alone only when I am in
the bathroom or in my bedroom.

If I am around other people it may make them uncomfortable if I touch myself anywhere down in my pants.

This may make people not like me! If people do not like me they will not want to play with me.

If I need to touch myself in these places I should probably go somewhere where I can be alone.

People also may not want to play with me if
they see me putting my finger up my nose.

If I need to put my finger up my nose I should
probably do this only when I am all alone.

Here are some places I can touch myself when
I am around others.

5

Not touching

Some people do not want to be
touched. That is okay.

If I do not want to be touched I should
say, "Please don't touch me."

No one should ever touch me if I tell them not to.

If I tell someone not to touch me and they keep touching me I should tell my parent, my teacher, or another adult all about it.

No matter who the person is or what they say I should tell my parent, my teacher, or another adult all about it.

I should never touch a stranger or let a stranger touch me. I should never even talk to strangers.

I should not try to touch anyone who
is not my friend.

If a friend asks me not to touch
them I should not touch them.

If I touch a friend who does not want to be touched they may not want to be my friend.

If my parent or teacher tells me not to touch someone I need to be sure I do not touch them.

I should never touch anyone who does not want
to be touched...even if they are my friend.

6
Having my picture taken

A lot of people
take pictures with
cameras and phones
and video cameras.

No one should ever take my picture if I tell them not to. No one should ever video me if I tell them not to.

I should never let a person take a picture of me when I don't have all my clothes on.

I should always tell my parent, my teacher, or another adult if anyone takes a picture or video of me.

Keeping Children with Special Needs Safe

Information for Adults

This is a storybook with six stories presented in a format designed to be highly accessible and more easily understood by children with developmental delays and cognitive disabilities. This book is written for young children and may not be appropriate for adolescents or adults.

The book has two primary purposes. First, it is a means to present information concerning some of the most common difficulties with touching others that many children with special needs experience (e.g. inappropriate hugging, hurting others, etc.). Together these six stories present a shotgun-style approach to tackling many of these behavioral difficulties by establishing a formal knowledge of some basic social norms regarding touching others for the child passing into school age.

Of course, a child possessing knowledge of social norms does not guarantee that he or she will adhere to them. The parent, teacher, or caregiver will often need to incentivize appropriate touching behaviors and discourage inappropriate touching behaviors. Manasco (2006) presents a novel system to show parents and teachers how to effectively discourage inappropriate behaviors and how to incentivize replacement behaviors in a book entitled *The Way to A*.

The second purpose of this book, which is as important as teaching children with special needs how to touch others, is to endow children with special needs with knowledge regarding the social norms of other people touching them. Children with special needs constitute one of our most vulnerable populations and are two to three times more likely to be maltreated than children without disabilities (Sullivan and Knutson, 2000). Specifically, children with autism are seven times more likely to be abused than non-disabled peers (Sullivan and Knutson, 2000). In 2001 the American Academy of Pediatrics stated that children with disabilities are at heightened risk of abuse because they have limited access to "critical information pertaining to personal safety" (p.509) concerning physical abuse. Mayer and Brenner (1989) stated that disabled children may lack the opportunity to learn what is normal in social interactions. As a result these children are often unable to recognize physical abuse when it occurs. This book is written to help parents and teachers begin to fill this void of knowledge on the part of the child.

Embedded within these six stories is the information every child needs to understand and carry with them. No single story is set apart to target physical abuse overtly. Rather, all six stories work together to create an explicit knowledge of what is and isn't appropriate with regards to touch. The stories also establish for children what to do if someone does touch them in a way that they believe is inappropriate. The "what to do" message is simple and repeated throughout the text. It is to "tell an adult." The adults specifically named are "parent" or "teacher" since these are usually the representatives of a child's two primary environments—home and school. Naturally, these are probably the people a child will be most comfortable with. Nonetheless, a third option is presented of "another adult" so as not to constrain a child or keep them from approaching any other adult they feel comfortable with. For the children capable of understanding, it should be emphasized that if one adult does not believe them when they report possible abuse, they should find and tell another adult.

More often than not, the abuser of a child is a caregiver. Since children with special needs often have multiple caregivers there is a higher chance of abuse. However, because there are multiple caregivers the abuse inflicted by one caregiver is more likely to be recognized by another. Educating the child, being explicit with other caregivers and educators about physical and sexual abuse, and letting it be known that the child is educated on what is and isn't appropriate behavior all provide powerful deterrents for any abuse. It is also important to teach caregivers of a child with special needs how to spot signs of abuse.

Be direct and upfront about what you expect from those responsible for your children or the students in your care, and tell them that you talk regularly with the child about how others should and shouldn't be touching them. Show this book around and let it be known that you, your child, and other caregivers have a plan in place for the recognition and reporting of possible physical and sexual abuse.

Indicators of possible child abuse

Because primary caregivers, teachers, and child care workers all spend a good deal of time with the children they care for, they are able to closely observe them from day to day and week to week. This opportunity for close observation places these individuals in a good position to identify possible child abuse. Although knowing what to look for is important in detecting abuse, one must be careful when checking for indicators of abuse. Goldman (1995) emphasizes that no single sign of abuse should be interpreted as a guarantee of abuse. However, if indicators of abuse occur frequently the observer needs to be alert to possible maltreatment or abuse. Hibbard, Desch, and the American Academy of Pediatrics' Committee on Child Abuse and Neglect (2011) suggest that because abuse and maltreatment in children with disabilities is often difficult to identify "a high index of suspicion in selected cases is warranted" (p.1021).

There are many varying lists of indicators of possible abuse. Some are quite exhaustive, but the box that follows contains a fairly concise list of physical, behavioral, and environmental indicators of possible abuse.

INDICATORS OF ABUSE

Physical indicators

- unexplained bruises, burns, cuts, or abrasions
- human bite marks
- torn or bloody clothing
- unexplained skeletal or internal injuries
- unexplained missing or loosened teeth
- unexplained head injuries

Behavioral indicators

- frightened by parents or caregivers
- fearful/wary of physical contact
- wears long sleeve clothing to hide injuries
- fearful of certain places, people, or activities
- eating and sleeping problems
- acting out inappropriate sexual behaviors
- premature understanding of sex
- aggressive or rebellious behavior
- extreme mood swings, withdrawal, excessive crying
- absence of positive self-image

Environmental indicators

- conflict between caregivers
- conflict between parent and child
- substance abuse of caregivers
- unemployment of caregivers
- inadequate child protection resources
- vague child abuse laws and policies
- social and geographical isolation of family
- overcrowding in the home

Physical indicators involve the child's appearance. *Behavioral indicators* involve characteristics of the child's behavior. *Environmental indicators* are known conditions that predispose a child to abuse or neglect. Identifying abuse in children with special needs is notoriously difficult, though it is certainly possible even in cases of severely autistic children, as displayed by Howlin and Clements (1995). It should be noted that many of the physical, behavioral, and social disabilities present in children with special needs may naturally resemble signs of abuse. An example presented by Hibbard and Desch (2011) is of children with motor and balance difficulties who often experience more bumps and bruises than a normal child due to their difficulty physically navigating their environment without accidents.

If a child confides to you that he or she is being abused

If a child reports abuse to you, you should not investigate or contact the alleged abuser. Be sure to document everything the child says carefully, provide a safe environment for the child, and immediately report the situation to your local law enforcement and child protective services agency. For more information, or if you do not know who to contact, see below for agencies with helplines which can direct you appropriately.

Where to get help if you are or were abused
IN THE UNITED STATES, ITS TERRITORIES, OR CANADA

If you are being abused or you need to report abuse in the United States, its territories, or Canada, you can contact **Childhelp** at 1-800-442-4453 any day, at any time of the day. You can also visit the Childhelp website for more information at www.childhelp.org.

You may also visit **Adult Survivors of Child Abuse (ASCA)** at http://ascasupport.org for information or support if you were abused or they can be called directly at (415) 928-4576.

IN THE UNITED KINGDOM

In the United Kingdom you may visit the website for **The National Association for People Abused in Childhood** at www.napac.org.uk for information or call them at 0800 085 3330.

You may also visit the website for the **National Society for the Prevention of Cruelty to Children** at www.nspcc.org.uk or call their helpline at 0800 1111 for children and young people and at 0808 800 5000 for adults concerned about a child.

References

Goldman, R.L. (1995). Recognizing child abuse and neglect in child care settings. *Day Care and Early Education, 22*(3), 12–15.

Hibbard, R. and Desch, L. (2011). Maltreatment of children with disabilities. *Pediatrics, 119*(5), 1018–1025.

Howlin, P. and Clements, J. (1995). It is possible to assess the impact of abuse on children with pervasive developmental disorders? *Journal of Autism and Developmental Disorders, 25*(4), 337–353.

Kairys, S.W., Alexander, R.C., Block, R.W., Everett, V.D., Hymel, K.P. and Jenny, C. (2001). American Academy of Pediatrics: Assessment of maltreatment of children with disabilities. *Pediatrics, 108*(2), 508–512.

Manasco, H.M. (2006). *The Way to A: Empowering Children with Autism Spectrum and Other Neurological Disorders to Monitor and Replace Aggression and Tantrum Behavior.* Overland, KS: Autism Asperger Publishing Company.

Mayer, P. and Brenner, S. (1989). Abuse of children with disabilities. *Children's Legal Rights Journal, 16*(4), 16–20.

Sullivan, P.M. and Knutson, J.F. (2000). Maltreatment and disabilities: A population based epidemiological study. *Child Abuse and Neglect, 22*, 271–288.